Tł

Eco

Hilary Cooper

Oval Books

Published by Oval Books
335 Kennington Road
London SE11 4QE
United Kingdom

Telephone: +44 (0)20 7582 7123
Fax: +44 (0)20 7582 1022
E-mail: info@ovalbooks.com
Web site: www.ovalbooks.com

Series Editor – Anne Tauté

Cover designer – Vicki Towers
Cover image – © Corbis
Printer – Cox & Wyman Ltd.
Producer – Oval Projects Ltd.

The Bluffer's® Guides series is based
on an original idea by Peter Wolfe.

The Bluffer's Guide®, The Bluffer's Guides®,
Bluffer's®, and Bluff Your Way® are
Registered Trademarks.

Acknowledgement and thanks are given
to the originators of items on pp 56.

ISBN-13: 978-1-903096-46-8
ISBN-10: 1-903096-46-4

CONTENTS

INTRODUCTION

In a world in which there is never enough to go round, and everyone wants a share of the action, economics tries to explain how societies organize themselves to square that circle. So, if pressed for a one-line explanation the bluffer could say that economics: "examines the allocation of scarce resources amongst competing wants".

What this means is that economics is all about competition, survival and that most basic of human emotions, greed. Think of small children fighting over a packet of sweets, or an older child ruthlessly bartering inferior sweets for the more desirable ones of a younger sibling, and you'll get the picture.

For the beginner in all this, economics will present a dazzling blend of jargon, bluster and breeze. In getting behind its façade, your task as a bluffer is to pick a few choice nuggets and flaunt them for all they are worth. As you do, hold in your mind that understanding economics is no more than a game in which your aim, as economist Joan Robinson once so eloquently put it, is not so much to find "a set of ready-made answers to economic questions" as to "avoid being deceived by economists".

UNDERSTANDING HOW ECONOMISTS THINK

Understanding how economists think is crucial to your whole enterprise. The beginning of good bluffing is to realize that economics is an abstract and often counter-intuitive subject. Any similarity it bears to real events, the real world or indeed to real people is therefore entirely co-incidental.

In order to master this art of abstraction, you first need to perfect the art of making 'assumptions'.

Assumptions

Economics seeks to simplify events and behaviour in the real world into a few 'laws', preferably ones that look good when expressed mathematically, because this immediately excludes about 90% (that's nine out of ten) of the population from understanding them. To do this, it makes use of assumptions. For instance, economists commonly assume that everyone has perfect information about prices, knowing through some kind of innate telepathy how much the same item costs in every place it is sold, which if any of them had actually ever been shopping they would know cannot be the case.

Oddly enough, economists will readily admit that the real world isn't really like this. It's just that they need to assume perfect information (temporarily, of course), in order to show how the economy works. Once this is achieved, the assumptions can be varied, or even relaxed altogether.

Having grasped that economics is all about suspending your disbelief, you will begin to understand the power of this tool. There need be no limit to your flights of fancy, providing that you avoid propositions that are too obviously preposterous (so pigs can fly is ruled out). Try the following:

The rationality principle
One of the most astonishing assumptions in economics, this asserts that human beings are basically rational and that all economic behaviour is therefore, by extension, also rational. Hence Rational Economic Man roams through the textbooks of economics, instantly making calculations and judgements about what sort of behaviour is in his best interests and what will maximize his happiness or 'utility' as it is known in the trade. Significantly, he has no female

counterpart, no Rational Economic Woman, perhaps because no-one would believe that any woman would be silly enough to behave like this.

So important is rationality in economics that a dedicated sect (known as the Chicago School) has developed it into the idea of Rational Expectations. This theory holds not just that all behaviour is rational, but that all the rational players in the economy know exactly what is going to happen in the future because they know that everyone else is rational – rather like a game of chess where everyone is a Grand Master.

Of course the great advantage of making this particular assumption is that as an entirely self-contained, rational system the economy can be represented ('modelled' to the bluffer) by a lot of very complicated mathematical equations. This is because maths, unlike people, is rational.

Equilibrium

Once mathematically-inclined economists got hold of the rationality principle, they were then able to develop a whole branch of economics that showed what would happen if you also assumed that the world was perfect (a small additional step once you have assumed that everyone is rational).

You begin by assuming a world in which everyone is either a producer trying to make as much money as possible (that's 'profit maximising behaviour', as you will soon effortlessly recognise) or a buyer trying to pull off the best possible deal that he can get (that's 'utility maximizing', naturally). As everyone is rational, no other types of behaviour are allowed. Add to this the assumption that everyone has all the information they need (that's 'perfect information') and degree level skills in maths to compute their next move, and you have the foundations of **General Equilibrium** theory.

3

When an economy is in equilibrium everything works like clockwork, with each part of its complicated mechanism in balance with the rest, and automatic adjustments coming into play whenever the balance gets disrupted. For the mathematician this has the added attraction that it can easily be modelled with a few hundred simultaneous equations.

Economists do, of course, recognize that some of these balancing adjustments may take time, because not everything is perfect all the time – the clockwork mechanism is subject to a certain amount of friction. Nevertheless, subscribers to the theory claim that eventually – 'in the long run' – these adjustments will always take place. So, for instance, massive widespread unemployment would in this analysis be a temporary period of 'disequilibrium' to be righted in due course by some fortuitous adjustment process. So long as the theory can be salvaged, no-one really need be bothered about how equilibrium is restored or what, in practice, 'the long-run' actually means.

It took the great economist John Maynard Keynes to produce a genuinely telling critique of such ideas. All bluffers should be familiar with what is probably the most remarkable insight in the history of economic analysis, and be able to repeat Keynes's immortal observation that, "In the long run we are all dead."

Ceteris paribus

No respectable academic subject wants to be without its Latinisms, and economics is no exception. Ceteris Paribus is the assumption to beat all assumptions and this is the bluffer's pièce de resistance, particularly when cornered by those who do not understand the abstractions of economics.

Translated as 'other things being equal' this has the equivalent status for the economist that the small print in a

4

legal contract has for the lawyer. It means that if anything whatsoever that the economist didn't know or care about causes his argument to be wrong, then it's still right anyway.

So, you might argue that, Ceteris Paribus, house prices are going to fall through the floor next year, or that on-line shopping will never catch on with the over-60s. The argument is irrelevant really. The key technique is to be ready, when confronted with the evidence that you were wrong, to call Ceteris Paribus to your aid. Other things did not remain constant. The banking institutions cut interest rates and artificially generated a house price boom. The internet companies caught on to the idea of larger type. With nifty footwork you can always find something or someone who moved the goalposts. It doesn't make your theory wrong. Hindsight has nowhere to hide when confronted with Ceteris Paribus.

So how did economics arrive at this rarefied state of argument? Let's meet a few of the famous.

THE ALL TIME GREATS

Adam Smith (1723-90)
Often considered the father of economics, Adam Smith introduced the concept of the Invisible Hand, which in an omniscient, omnipresent sort of way would intervene to make everything in the economy run smoothly. This was a convenient early assumption which justified politicians keeping well away from any attempt at managing the economy. Indeed the theory counselled against such interference since the near divine workings of the Invisible Hand would clearly deliver better results than meddling by mere mortals. The seminal concept of laissez faire (leave well

alone) follows from this analysis, and remains the buttress of economic conservatives today. Bluffers should make sure they drop the term into the conversation – whether disparagingly or not will depend on the stance you have decided to adopt (q.v.).

Thomas Malthus (1766-1834)

In some ways the Eeyore of the early political economists, Malthus developed to dizzy new heights the Hobbesian concept that life is nasty, brutish and short. Thus he asserted that in a world of finite resources the rapid increase in population that accompanied industrialization would inevitably lead to shortages, starvation, death and eventual cosmic obliteration. (So, not unlike today's Green party). But the upside for Malthus was that this would have the effect of reducing the size of the population, bringing it back into equilibrium with its resource base. For the bluffer, the key point to latch on to is that a Malthusian approach to economics entails doom-laden prophesies of impending disaster likely to receive about as much attention as the prophesies of Cassandra in ancient Greece.

David Ricardo (1772-1823)

Ricardo, a man with a fondness for lists, came up with the idea of economic rent (how much you can extract from others by dint of holding an asset). This he artfully linked to one of those convenient conceptual frameworks beloved of economics teachers, the notion that there are three basic building blocks in an economy: land, labour and capital, which, as he showed, provide their proud possessors with rent, wages and profits. Collectively known as the 'factors of production' – no self-respecting bluffer's repertoire is complete without being able to recite this mantra.

Karl Marx (1818-1883)

Marx focused on the ownership of the factors of production, with land and capital (money and machinery) being in the hands of nasty 'capitalists' who used their wealth and power to exploit the 'working classes' who owned nothing but their own labour. Primarily an historian, Marx propounded the historical inevitability of class conflict and the revolutionary overthrow of capitalism by the masses. Had he witnessed the joining of forces between capitalism and the people in mass consumerism and global phenomena such as McDonald's, he would no doubt have turned in his Highgate grave.

Léon Walras (1834-1910)

Inspiration for ballads by Lewis Carol and John Lennon, in real life Walras got his teeth into something far more surreal: the mathematical proof of general equilibrium – perhaps the ultimate in mind-altering states.

Alfred Marshall (1842-1924)

A somewhat more sedate economist firmly rooted in the 'classical' school which enshrines the principles of order, harmony and perfection within the economics discipline. Slightly wilder early on in his career when he ran amok with a pair of scissors, using the open blades to demonstrate how supply and demand intersect to determine prices, he settled down after discovering that graph paper would do the job just as well. Most of his later work then became a rather tedious form of micro-economics concerned with equilibrium, why marginal utility and prices are the same thing and other more or less imaginary concepts, so unless you enjoy calculus or want to be a teacher, you can safely avoid this subject as nobody is ever likely to want to discuss it with you.

Francis Edgeworth (1845-1926)
Remembered only for inventing the Edgeworth Box whose main distinction has been to perplex successive generations of economics students. The salient point for the bluffer to remember is that the box is full of 'indifference curves', which are one of the more baffling concepts of micro-economics. These curves are essentially graphs which show the points at which one is indifferent between two things: another apple versus another pear, an extra hour of pay versus an extra hour of leisure, watching *Big Brother* or going to bed. You get the idea. Quite impressive to drop into the conversation, but don't expect an enthusiastic response.

Vilfredo Pareto (1848-1923)
Worth mentioning for his early contribution to welfare economics – the study of who gets what and who decides who gets what. He left us with the concept of 'Pareto optimality', a sublime condition (which may or may not exist) in which no-one can be made better off without someone else being made worse off. Pareto declared that once this state of nirvana is reached, no further changes would be needed to the way things are dished out. Of no interest of course to the large bullying child who wants more sweets from a weaker companion.

John Maynard Keynes (1883-1946)
A colossus of the economics world, Keynes is one of the few economists to have become a household name. His revolution was to see the economy as akin to some kind of giant thermostat. When it gets a bit over-heated you can cool it down by raising taxes and cutting government expenditure to take the steam out of all that consumerism. This gives the government a bit of money in its back pocket which it can then use if things swing too far the other way and the

economy blows cold (as in a recession). At this point the government can warm everything up again by cutting taxes and increasing government spending.

Developed in response to the '30s Depression, Keynesianism was intended to deliver 'full employment', although the policy was caricatured by some as the government paying people to dig holes and then fill them in again. Ultimately, it suffered from the problems of most thermostatic control systems – you can never quite get the fine-tuning right. Hence the labelling of the period of Keynesian economic management (after the event) as the era of 'Stop-Go'.

The bluffer must have a view on Keynes, whether it be to admire his vision or to poo-poo his policies as a dated, or even a dangerous, leftish fad.

Joan Robinson (1903-83)
A Cambridge contemporary of both Marshall and Keynes, who become a leading light in the Cambridge Capital Controversy. The main feature of this debate was that absolutely nobody could understand it (although quite how it became a controversy in these circumstances is unclear). Again demonstrating the capacity of economics to bear little or no relation to the real world, Robinson's Capital Theory appears to assert that capital is incapable of being measured or of having a value. One for the esoterics, she is nevertheless considered one of the all time greats, cruelly denied a Nobel prize by a male economics establishment which either didn't dare admit it couldn't understand her work, or was afraid of its incipient Marxist tendencies.

Milton Friedman (1912)
Friedman is the architect of the other major theory of economic management – Monetarism. Operating in direct opposition to Keynesianism, Friedman argued that messing

around with taxes and spending (fiscal policy to the bluffer) could not bring economic stability, and that the only effective strategy was the use of monetary policy – control of the money supply and interest rates. The key objective of Monetarists is to keep the lid on inflation by regulating the amount of money in circulation – rather like rationing a child's pocket money to stop them spending it all at once. The fact that this has the effect of putting sweet shops out of business and creating a few million unemployed, is generally considered to be less important than controlling inflation.

Amartya Sen (1933)

Sen's contribution to economics has been to turn the spotlight on how wealth, income and economic power are shared out. Taking the novel step of applying philosophical ideas to the arena of political economy, he came up with the idea of 'entitlement' to basic economic well-being. This argues that it isn't enough for there to be food, housing and other basic essentials available in the shop window, as it were, if the people who need them do not have the economic clout (money or jobs) to get them. By forcing would-be policy makers to confront the paradox of resource-rich countries harbouring desperately poor people, Sen provided a strong rebuttal to the 'let them eat cake' branch of political economy.

As you can see there is plenty of room to champion your own pet economists, real or imaginary, although the safest ones are always those who are either a) ground-breaking or b) dead. Still you should not underestimate the power of the familiar: a good, solid name like Johnston can be trotted out when occasion demands, e.g: "As Johnston says..." or "According to Johnston's Law..." (no-one will care to admit they have never heard of any such theory). Or simply adjust your choice to the nationality of your companion: Malinvaud (mal-in-voe) is a good one for the French, Leijonhufvud (layon-her-fud) for the Nordic states, and perhaps Kalecki (kal-let-ski) if you meet a Pole, with whom you can sympathize over his nation's tragic history by lamenting the fact that Kalecki had both the great good fortune to have simultaneously with Keynes invented The General Theory (as bluffers must casually call it), allied to the great misfortune to have written it in Polish.

MASTERING THE BASICS

Now that you have met some of the the key influences on the development of economic thought, it is time to get down to the basics and familiarize yourself with some underlying concepts. Economics began life as the Greek term *okos nemo*, meaning house rules, or household management, so where better to start than with the shopping (or 'the market' as economists like to call it).

How markets work

The economy is basically a system of interlocking markets, so understanding how they work is a pretty good idea. To bluff convincingly you need to be able to describe markets using the appropriate terms. Take a conventional market stall selling bananas, a classic example. Here the pile of bananas is **the supply**, and the queue of people wanting to buy the bananas makes up **the demand**.

If producers have correctly guessed how many bananas their consumers want at today's going rate then supply and demand will be in balance, rather like the two weights on either side of an old-fashioned set of scales. If something happens to upset this balance then prices will adjust up or down in order to re-balance the two forces of supply and demand. So when a banana seller looks as if he's going to be left with a pile of rotting bananas on a Saturday afternoon and starts yelling, "C'mon ladies*, ten for a pound", you will know that there is an excess supply and a dwindling demand. Economists will dress this up by saying that the producer is trying to find the 'market clearing price' – one that will of course be lower than the banana price at the start of the day.

At times the opposite will happen and there will be an excess demand – more people queuing for bananas than the market seller can possibly satisfy. In this case, if he has his wits about him, or has been to business school, the market clearing price will go up. The stall holder won't care if this annoys some consumers so they drop out of his queue, because he couldn't have supplied all of them anyway. When there is excess demand, he will only sell to those prepared to pay the higher price. This is known as 'profit maximising behaviour', or making a fast buck. It is playground stuff.

These simple principles – which are the essence of what is known as micro-economics – will stand you in good stead for talking about any kind of market, be it bananas, cars, currencies, or currant buns. However, the sophisticated bluffer might occasionally observe that not all markets operate quite as smoothly as the banana market where prices can easily go up or down to suit the circumstances.

In other, more complicated markets, like the labour market, prices – in this case wages – don't always adjust up and down to match supply and demand. That way lies potential starvation – a fact recognised if not always by employers, then certainly by trade unions and other forms of labour organisation, as well as governments, usually, although sometimes too late.

Societies will therefore have controls in place to stop

* It is a given in economics, and perhaps in life generally, that all consumers are female.

wages falling below a certain agreed level, meaning that the labour market is not a fully price-adjusting market. Instead it adjusts on quantity. So, when there are too many people looking for work (excess supply), rather than starvation wages there will be no wages, or unemployment, for those at the end of the queue. Unemployment benefits or relief will then come into play, as society's booby prize.

You need only observe that this is one of a number of instances where markets don't operate as the text books say they will, idiosyncrasies variously described as **market rigidities**, **market failures**, or **market imperfections**. There is no reason why you should be able to distinguish between the different types, as no-one else can. The important point to hang on to is that if Governments are going to start intervening in markets they need to be clear about what imperfections they are trying to correct. Hence the confident bluffer must always be prepared to challenge the advocate of any such policy to justify it on the basis of a specific market failure.

The macro economy

This complex tapestry of markets and transactions makes up the complete system known as 'The Economy'.

Much of economists' time is spent scrutinizing the economy, trying to predict its next move, wary that, like some dormant dinosaur, it will suddenly wake up and pounce on them. Their attempts to tame the beast feed the activity of **political economy**: making difficult choices between alternative courses of actions or, at the very least, making speeches that can be passed off as making difficult choices.

(As a bluffer, when discussing The Economy – the overall system – you should always refer to it as the **macro-economy**. This contrasts with the **micro-economy**, which you now know deals with detailed individual markets and transactions.)

When describing this system, economists often invest it with almost human-like qualities, calling it 'youthful' or 'mature', for instance. Youthful economies, like youths themselves, enjoy the great outdoors, being full of fields of waving corn and very little else. As they grow into a 'secondary' economy, ugly factories spring up like infected spots, obliterating the fields of corn, and all that youthful energy is poured into developing the manufacturing sector. Finally, as maturity sets in, and everyone has a bit more money but no energy left for manufacturing, the economy enters its third age. The mature economy is one where services predominate: taxis to take you to your chiropodist, complicated savings accounts to build up your wealth, and lawyers to ensure you pass it all on.

No modern economy has progressed beyond this third stage and on to death, although several have needed serious resuscitation or shown definite signs of regression.

The macro-economy, then, deals with aggregates – great sweeping generalizations and broad-brush sketches of the big picture. In discussing this subject the key macro-economic concepts of Output, Inflation, Unemployment and Taxation should trip off your tongue, although not necessarily all at the same time.

Output

1 What it is

Output, or national income as some traditionalists prefer to call it, is what is produced by all the feverish energy in the economy. Intuitively, output is pretty easy to understand. It is the potatoes dug from the ground, the cars that come off the production line, the haircut, the restaurant meal, the latest episode of *Dr Who*. All you have to do to know the output of the economy is to add all those things together. Easy enough, one might think.

But (as in life) there is a distinction between what is paid for and what is not, and the general rule is that if it is not paid for it won't be counted. This means that a wife can't consider the bookcase erected by her handyman husband as part of national output. Nor can he count her triumphs over blocked drains, greenfly or gravy. This arises because whilst everyone clearly knows (or at any rate thinks they know) the value of their unpaid work, economists are unable to count it because no money has changed hands and it therefore isn't in any accountant's ledger.

In some cases this happens even where money does change hands because it does so clandestinely or illicitly. Thus cash-in-hand payments to mechanics, builders, cleaners, drug dealers and dog-walkers get missed from measures of output, forming instead the informal, black or shadow economy. Generally estimated to be about 10% of all economic activity in the U.K., EU statisticians increased this figure to 50% when analyzing the Italian economy (although the Mafia later admitted that their accountant had been fiddling the books).

The situation is complicated further by second-hand goods which are also not recorded when sold. This could become more of a problem as nations increasingly turn to internet sites such as E-bay and people stop buying new products, and simply re-cycle things when they're bored with them. Indeed, you could hypothesize that the only area of economic output likely to rise in the future will be express delivery services.

2 How it is measured

Keeping all these caveats in mind, then, we come to the tricky business of actually measuring the small amount of activity that still counts as output. One can only assume that at some point the government must have tasked a committee to deal with this and that in the time-honoured fashion of such institutions it decided that it wouldn't do to come up with a single solution where several would do. So economics finds itself in a position where output can be measured in any of three possible ways:

1 by income;
2 by expenditure;
3 by 'value added'.

The next flash of inspiration was to give output a new name that no-one would recognize. Because nobody could agree what it should be, several were picked, each with a subtly different meaning, to be used at whim. Thus you have Gross Domestic Product (GDP), Gross National Product (GNP), Net Domestic Product, Net National Product and so on. Any of these can be measured at either 'factor cost' – how much all the different parties were paid for the final product – or 'market price' – what the output was finally sold for after taxes or subsidies had been added.

The result of this superb example of clarity and consensus in decision-making is that there is now a whole profession of statisticians employed solely to understand the difference between these measures (so jobs for life for them). This being the case, there is no need to agonise any further. When talking about output, stick firmly to GDP (at factor cost, if pressed) and challenge anyone who wants to use another measure to explain it first.

Growth

Output tells us what is produced by an economy, growth tells us how quickly that output is growing. Economies have a long-run or trend rate of growth (somewhere around 2% to 3% per annum is considered reasonable going for the more mature economies of the developed world, younger economies should do better than that). Around this trend rate, growth tends to fluctuate up and down in a fairly regular pattern, shown in graphs as a wave-like pattern, and known as the economic (or business) cycle. A complete economic cycle can last around 5-10 years and long-term (or trend) growth should therefore be measured by comparing the same points in successive cycles – 'peak to peak' being the convention.

During the upswing of a cycle growth will surge ahead of its trend, generating the happy feeling of boom times, only to be followed by the all too familiar bust as the bubble bursts. Like the wheel turning at the fair, this then puts the economy into a downswing, with growth now falling below trend. A number of things can happen next.

- If growth slows down, but does not actually stop, the economy is said to have had a soft landing.

- If output falls, so that growth is negative, economists call it a **recession**.

- If things get really bad, and no-one can see their way out of it, it will be given the more miserable epithet, **depression**.

Bluffers will find that measures of growth vie only with measures of per capita income (output per person) as virility tests for nations and their politicians. Hallowed organizations like the Organisation for Economic Co-operation and Development (OECD) and the World Bank produce league tables comparing and contrasting the performance of economies on these measures. Of course the fact that growth goes in cycles provides economists, statisticians and politicians with fertile ground for disputing any and all statistics on the matter. Thus growth could be low because it is 'below trend' or hasn't been measured 'peak to peak' or is 'at the downpoint' or (a more recent variant), because statisticians changed their minds about when the last economic cycle ended and the next one began.

Output and growth are both affected by the overall level of demand in the economy. This could be consumers demanding things to buy, investors demanding new machinery or capital goods, or governments demanding just about anything.

Economists spend a lot of time analyzing what causes demand to go up or down, trying to devise policies to influence things in the direction they want them to go. One way to do this is to tap into different groups' **marginal propensity to consume** (in plain English, how much you spend for every extra pound you're given). For most, the marginal propensity could go either way: an unexpected windfall could be blown on champagne or put aside for a weekend in Clacton-on-Sea. Pensioners, though, can be relied on to spend every penny they get. Hence Chancellors can cleverly conceal a last ditch attempt to stimulate the economy under the guise of a Christmas turkey handout for the elderly, effectively killing two old birds with one stone.

Savings

All of which brings us on neatly to that little-known indicator termed the **savings ratio**, a measure of how much of the nation's income is being saved rather than spent. Providing everyone isn't putting wodges of cash under the mattress, saving can perform a very useful economic function as the loot people fondly believe to be sitting safely in a savings account is in fact being invested by financial institutions behind their back. As long as they don't blow it, this should increase the size of the economic cake allowing everyone a bigger slice.

This helps explain why economists tend to become rather

alarmed if the savings ratio dips too low, particularly if people not only stop saving but start to borrow money they don't have, as is increasingly the case, creating the new spectre of the 'negative savings ratio', or just plain debt. If and when savings are low, you will suddenly find the government offering all sorts of silly-sounding savings schemes (TESSAs, ISAs) supposed to encourage the population to put more of their readies away. You might care to suggest that the government would do better to invest in the only proven way to conquer that urge to spend – a compulsory course of hypnosis.

Inflation

Inflation, or more accurately, price inflation, is another of those macro-economic variables that economists like to fuss over. Inflation is measured by the Consumer Prices Index (CPI), or one of its many faddish approximations, which takes the idea of a shopper's basket of goods to measure how the price of a standard set of goods changes from month to month. No-one seems to have told the Office for National Statistics that people use carrier bags these days.

An annual rate of inflation above about 2%-3% is generally considered a bad thing because it creates a lot of uncertainty, makes it hard for business to plan, and generally erodes the value of earnings and any savings that people may have. (Note that, as usual in economics, this downside has its flip side: since it devalues debt too, high inflation is a dream come true for those with large mortgages.)

Much of policy-makers' time is spent trying to keep inflation low and, in support of this economists agonise over the causes of any given episode, with Monetarists having particularly strong views on the matter (q.v.). To hold your own in this debate, you should know that inflation can be one of two types – 'demand pull' and 'cost push'.

Demand pull occurs when too much money is chasing too few goods, and (as in the auction of a rare Picasso) prices go through the roof. It occurs classically during wars when factories switch from producing armchairs to armaments, and too few people are farming the land so that, without some form of rationing, inflation rockets.

Cost push, by contrast, comes from increases in production costs (raw materials becoming more expensive, labour costs rising or even just general 'red tape'). These forces tend to interact – if the cost of inputs rises and producers put their prices up, employees will bargain for higher wages, causing producers to put prices up further, degenerating into a tit for tat spat that rejoices in the name of 'cost push inflationary spiral'.

So much for the overview of the complete system. It's time to look at the key drivers of economic activity and growth – businesses, the workforce and trade.

Competition – survival of the fittest

It is businesses which produce the output of the economy and in the cut-throat world of economic competition they will only survive if they can produce what customers want at a price they are prepared to pay, and nobble the competition in the process. Businesses are generally set up by entrepreneurs – go-getters who spot market opportunities and are prepared to take risks to exploit them.

If they are successful and the business takes off, entrepreneurs will often sell out to a team of smart-suited executives who will finance further business expansion by selling shares (equity to you) possibly, though not necessarily, through a stock market flotation. Bluffers should be aware that **entrepreneurship** is now known as the fourth factor of production (after land, labour and capital). So crucial is it to success that a group of American tycoons has kindly offered to translate the word into French to support that nation's indifferent economy.

Those with a penchant for the petite may cling to the belief that small is beautiful, but it has to be recognized that many enterprises, particularly in manufacturing, benefit from being built on an altogether larger scale. If you're going to have to pay for a whacking great piece of machinery, plus your marketing and finance department, staff tearoom, tinsel at Christmas, you might as well churn out as much as you possibly can to defray such fixed costs, preferably keeping the whole shooting match going all night long as well if you have any respect for capital utilisation. Anyone operating on this grand stage will reap what the bluffer will know are **Economies of Scale**.

Once businesses have established themselves they may, like children who want to keep others out of their game, try and protect their position by becoming a **monopoly** business – the only supplier in the market – or, if slightly less successful, an **oligopoly** – one of a very small number of suppliers. The bluffer will know that both are generally considered to be a bad thing because in the absence of effective competition these businesses can charge what they like for their products, so that survival of the fittest gives way to fat cats who get all the cream. Governments will therefore attempt to regulate monopoly businesses, seeking to free up markets to competition, and, in so far as market globalisation will permit, clamping down on attempts by large conglomerates to use mergers and take-overs to create monopolies by stealth.

One way that businesses, industries and economies push ahead is through **innovation** – the successful exploitation of new ideas – viz that epoch-changing invention, the microchip. However, as the famous American economist J.K. Galbraith once remarked, "It is easy to overlook the absence of appreciable advance in an industry. Innovations that are not made, like babies that are not born, are rarely missed."

Businesses also rely for their survival on others. The car manufacturer buys components from the small-scale metal manufacturer who in turn will source raw materials elsewhere. Similar to the food chain of the jungle, the bluffer will know this as the 'supply chain' of the market. As warehousing costs have increased and new technologies have made stock control so much more efficient, suppliers now practice 'just in time' delivery of inputs to their customers further up the supply chain, or, more likely, as the weary shopper will know, just too late, delivery.

Many businesses find it worthwhile to temper aggression and competition with more co-operative and mutually supportive behaviour. By forming into 'clusters' of similar types, located together, they all benefit from sharing information, expertise and biscuits (but only on Fridays). The well-informed bluffer will know that research by the American economist Michael Porter, and others, shows that such behaviour may in fact be more conducive to survival and success than 'naked' competition – however attractive the latter may sound to some.

The labour market – how people fit in

Employers need people to work in their businesses and, as a general rule, people need to work in order to live (although the odd few appear to have their priorities the other way round). This, then, gives you the basis of the labour market – jobs.

The bluffer will recognize that, like people, jobs come in different shapes and sizes: professional, skilled, unskilled, manual, non-manual, full-time, part-time, permanent, temporary and so on. Most people don't bother trying to get their heads round these fine distinctions because in practice the labour market is as segregated ('segmented' to you) as the American Deep South once was. Women or people without qualifications will be in unskilled or low-status jobs, probably temporary and frequently part-time, with poor earnings and few perks of the pensions and paid holidays kind. Men or the highly-qualified get all the other jobs, which they like to refer to as 'real' jobs (the implication being that all the others are somehow imaginary).

Jobs pay wages, otherwise no-one would bother working (with the exception of course of mothers, housewives and other unpaid carers engaged in a lifetime of martyrdom). How much you get paid really depends on how much your skills are worth, and how much value you produce for your employer (although stroppy trade unions can also give you a bit of an extra leg up the earnings ladder).

A smart move, then, is to build up a bit of 'human capital' by investing in education or training – the extra earning power that this gives you being the return on your investment. As with any such venture, some investments give a better rate of return than others. A year out in business school is generally considered one of the better flutters – more lucrative, say, than three years at teacher training college living on lentil soup.

Anyone of working age who either has a job (the employed) or is looking for a job (the unemployed) is considered **economically active** (and, yes, that does include those welded to their mobiles). All the others are, by definition, **economically inactive**. This includes:

- students (who are active, but not economically),
- parents of young children (who fantasize about having a day job but can't afford the childcare),
- those with health problems,
- a group known as discouraged workers, who have stopped looking for work in the belief that they will never get a job,

- the lucky few who simply have too much money to be bothered with work.

If things are working well, there will be enough jobs for the people who want them and employers will be able to meet their needs for qualified staff without hitting skills shortages, or skills mismatches (where workers have skills for which there are no jobs, and employers have jobs for which there are no skilled workers, leading to a phenomenon known as **structural unemployment**). In the fantasy scenario of full employment, there is only what is known as **frictional unemployment** – a few unemployed people rubbing along together for a short time as they move between jobs.

Back in the real world, unemployment has rarely been at the 2%-3% frictional level. This is at least in part because, unfortunately for the workforce, economists developed the idea that there is a trade-off between unemployment and inflation – when one is low the other is high. Hence when the deflating of inflation rises up the political agenda governments tend to allow unemployment to rise in the hope of drawing the sting from inflationary wage demands.

This is all fertile ground for the bluffer, who will know that the first articulation of this trade off is the **Phillips Curve** (though you should gently hint at not being fully convinced by Phillips' scatter diagrams), and rapidly move on to discuss the merits of the **NAIRU** (Non-Accelerating Inflation Rate of Unemployment).

Refuse to be drawn on the technical mathematical issues, sticking instead to the intuitive power of this idea, which basically states that there is a unique rate of unemployment that, for any given economy at any given time, will stop inflation taking off. Thus it has been argued by those who believe it, and you can always find at least one economist who will believe anything, that governments who pursue policies to reduce unemployment below this level do so at their peril.

The beauty of the whole idea for the bluffer is that no-one knows what the level of the NAIRU actually is, and in any case, it is always changing. What economists generally acknowledge, though, is that well functioning labour markets will tend to get away with lower unemployment (maybe nearer to 5% than 10%) before hitting the inflationary highspots, than more rigid ones in which a small group of workers is ruling the roost. Hence the preoccupation of many governments with **labour market flexibility**, which goes something like this:

Carrots:

a Take the jobs to the people, instead of the people to the jobs;

b Get more people working by giving in-work benefits to families that are better than being on the dole;

c Give people the wherewithal to get back to work, be it crèches, or crash courses, and then make sure they go;

d Get as many students and workers as possible trained in the skills of the future so that no-one can hold you over a barrel for higher wages.

Sticks:

a Don't let the unemployed rest – make sure they are out there looking for work;

b Don't let anyone get away with inactivity – particularly get rid of perks such as early retirement deals;

c Stop employers from discriminating against people with blue rinses or nose-rings;

d Whatever happens, don't let trade unions hold you over a barrel for higher wages.

The idea is that achieve this and you will have an efficiently functioning and flexible labour market in which low unemployment can co-exist with low inflation. By now, the bluffer will be well prepared for the degree of the abstract in economics, and will have no difficulty with the necessary suspension of disbelief required to imagine the above.

Trade – the final frontier

Siblings, tribes and nations have from time immemorial engaged in mutual trade. The bartering of animal skins for precious metals or the swapping of rare football cards, or footballers themselves for ready cash are all instances of this most basic instinct.

The bluffer will of course know that what is traded and at what price is driven by **comparative advantage**. Two countries may produce equally good cotton shirts at roughly the same price, but one may produce haute couture silk ties more cheaply than the other. The one with a comparative advantage in ties will therefore produce and export these, leaving the job of producing cotton shirts to the other, from whom they will import. If they can all find a third country with a comparative advantage in trousers this will not only guarantee that everyone gets an outfit at price they can afford, but that they can all go out without being arrested.

Although trade began as direct bartering of goods, as economic behaviour became more sophisticated people decided that coins were easier to handle than, say, carcasses. This transformed trade. The one mistake that was made was to let every country have its own currency, so each one has to have a rate of exchange in every other.

Quite apart from the resulting **transaction costs** – a term specially coined for any nuisance activity in economics such as currency exchange – governments are obliged to spend untold time and effort trying to adjust and fine tune their exchange rates to suit their economy. Bluffers should be able to recognize the jargon used to describe the plethora of regimes for exchange rate management that come and go: fixed, floating, pegged, snaked, charmed ...

The reason all this matters is that governments have to make sure that the country is spending approximately as much on imports as it receives from exports. If it gets this wrong there will be a **balance of payments** crisis – akin to your own when your monthly income is not enough to cover what you appear to have spent in the last four weeks.

One way of doing this is simply to impose 'import controls' to restrict foreign goods coming into the country, thereby protecting the home country's producers by using 'tariffs' – taxes that are slapped on the top of imported goods – or 'quotas' such as the limits placed on imports of cheap Chinese underwear that led to the infamous 'Bra Wars'.

Where governments cannot use such **protectionism** to cocoon their economy, they can manipulate their exchange rate instead, providing they haven't been foolish enough to give up control by fixing it to other currencies or, even more extreme, joining a common currency regime. In doing so they will have to weigh up the balance between:

- A 'strong' currency, with a high or even over-valued exchange rate in which interest rates are high (attracting investors to buy the currency). In this scenario imports are cheap, pleasing the population who can buy even more iPods and DVD players, but exports are expensive for other countries, displeasing businesses who find it hard to shift their goods. Since this means that people buy more, but businesses sell less, the balance of payments will go into the red, and something will need to give.

- A 'weak' currency, with a low, possibly under-valued, currency, pleasing businesses because selling abroad is

27

now cheaper, but obviously less popular with consumers and liable to stoke inflation in the economy unless everyone is persuaded to switch to home-produced goods – never as attractive, of course. Weak currencies do, though, generally lead to an improved balance of payments.

Note that when currency devaluation is used by governments to solve their problems in competing on the world stage, usually symptomatic of some deeper structural problem in the economy, what it does is benefit the devaluing country's businesses at the expense of foreign businesses. It's a practice that has therefore come to be known as exporting unemployment, or, less politely, beggar your neighbour.

The final spectre for any government in controlling its exchange rate would be a flight from the currency by quick-witted speculators looking to make a fast buck. This is an outcome to be avoided at all costs – a run on the currency is far worse than the effects of any other form of laxative.

Is it all a game?

Once economists had got going with their analysis of how people behave in the market place – and why – they began to notice how much it resembled a game. Strategy, tactics, the double or even triple bluff all give players in this psychological drama the edge they need to succeed. This led them to devise a game of their own: a new mathematical tool, helpfully called Game Theory, which could be used, as if playing God, to describe and predict how economic players would behave in different circumstances.

Ambitious bluffers should be at ease using terms like 'free rider' and 'zero sum game' (see Glossary) to denote the somewhat arcane practice of reducing human motivation to mathematical models. They should also be familiar with the parable of the **Prisoners' Dilemma** – one of, if not the, most useful insight to come out this branch of economic theorising.

Consider the scenario. Two suspects are arrested and interrogated in separate cells. Each is given these choices:

1 If one of you co-operates, confesses and betrays the other you will secure your own release and the other will be executed.
2 If both of you confess you will get long sentences, but not death because at least you co-operated.
3 If neither of you confesses you will serve a term in prison (though not for long, due to lack of proof).

It is evident that, faced with this choice, it is too risky for you or the other prisoner to stay loyal because, if you are ratted on, you face certain death.

Naturally there would be no game if everyone were altruistic, but self-interest being the stronger motive, both prisoners will choose to betray.

The irony is that if both could have trusted or even colluded with the other and chosen not to betray, the punishment would have been much less. The clear moral is that what is rational for an individual acting in isolation makes him worse off than he would have been had he been willing to make a co-operative decision. All this is handily expressed by game theorists in a chart called the pay-off matrix, identical to the one it is assumed will automatically form in the minds of any prisoners who happen to find themselves in this unfortunate position – although it is not recommended territory for bluffers.

Unusually, this parable has all sorts of clever applications in economics, which you may care to drop into convenient gaps in the conversation. For instance, cartels, such as the OPEC one to maintain high oil prices, is based on co-operative mutual decision making, in which all OPEC producers are better off by fixing the price of oil high. If just one member country were to defect and cut its price it would make a killing because no-one in their right mind would buy oil from any other country. This of course creates pressure for all countries to secretly cut the price. Should this happen it would of course make them all worse off as they would be selling in the same market at a lower price – the classic Prisoners' Dilemma.

FROM THEORY TO POLICY

The Multi-Headed Monster

It's all very well understanding how the economy works in theory, but ultimately someone has to put it all into practice. In the U.K. there are six heads to this hydra, and we shall start with:

1 The Chancellor of the Exchequer

The Chancellor of the Exchequer (a position equivalent to first minister of finance) makes the big decisions on macro-economic policy:

- how the economy is run,
- how much is spent on public services,
- who pays what in taxes,
- how much to put aside for the PM's phone bill.

To get the right balance requires the skill of a tightrope walker. Not doing so will bring forth the wrath of the rich and powerful at being forced to pay extra taxes, the consternation of the business community if inflation cannot be controlled, and the revenge of the electorate if the economy doesn't grow fast enough to provide serried ranks of satellite dishes staring down at squeaky-clean streets.

In the event that the Chancellor gets all, or even some, of his decisions right and the Exchequer coffers are full, he will reluctantly give money to other Ministers for their shopping lists of schools, hospitals and those old favourites, submarines and missiles. Each year there is a big media and political circus around 'The Budget', and more recently the Pre-Budget Report (PBR) where the Chancellor sets out his plans for the economy and, much more important, for the tax to be levied on whisky or whippets.

Sometimes Chancellors suffer from 'shocks' – such as a turn for the worse in the world economy, unpredictable hikes in prices of key raw materials (usually oil), a war, or some scandalous company cover-up. Or the one when they realise that they don't control everything after all. Although difficult to deal with if they knock the Chancellor's predictions off course, shocks are also very convenient scapegoats (of the Ceteris Paribus kind) for Chancellors who aren't delivering. They can therefore be used as a sort of economic equivalent of 'the dog ate my homework'.

2 The City

The City – an umbrella term for London's financial institutions – acts like a weather vane of confidence in how well the Chancellor is up to the job of managing the economy. The City will bend with the wind, however light the breeze, with speculators throwing their toys out of the pram (behaviour euphemistically referred to by Keynes as 'animal spirits') as soon as they see a threat to economic growth or stability. City tantrums tend to involve widespread selling of shares or holdings in whatever company, commodity or currency is thought to be vulnerable. This can create a de-stabilising environment for the Chancellor and, as with most tantrum management, can lead to short-term responses that pacify the City rather than more thought-through long-term solutions.

It has been known for the City to throw a wobbly simply because a particular political party looks likely to win the next General Election. However political parties are wise to this now and have got rid of any economic policies that could possibly tip the City over the edge.

3 The trade unions

Representing the interest of the workforce, trade unions have the capacity to bring large swathes of the economy to a standstill through the withdrawal of their labour, causing governments to try and scupper their activities with cleverly crafted pieces of industrial relations' legislation.

As a result, many of the unions' traditional concerns over issues such as the time that the last man to leave switches off the light are now just as likely to be enforced through that new instrument of torture, the EU Directive. Hence, governments can now spend long nights with Eurocrats at expensive dinners in Brussels thrashing out agreements to limit the perceived damage of costly new forms of labour protection, instead of doing it in their own backyard in the old-fashioned beer and sandwiches way.

4 The advisers

Even the most conscientious Chancellors cannot be expected to spend all day mugging up on economic theory or flicking through the latest sensationalist reports on the state of the economy. They therefore employ advisers to do this for them – such as the one, named Balls, who supplied the delightful phrase Neo-classical Endogenous Growth Theory (a.k.a. a load of ...).

Advisers are of course the brightest and best of their generation – economic advisers to the government have included Keynes and a roll call of future Nobel prize-winners. As with all such positions, though, the real role of the adviser is to take the flak when things don't go well, and stay out of the limelight when they do.

5 The pundits

For Chancellors, pundits are a bit like having an extra mother-in-law. They will offer unsolicited advice on any subject whether they know anything about it or not. Pundits can be academics (who have the advantage of being assumed to know what they are talking about), journalists (to whom the opposite applies) or independent analysts or commentators (who very probably do know a thing or two).

As with mothers-in-law, pundits will unerringly choose the most embarrassing timing and public forum for offering their advice, as well as having the most irritating knack of almost always being right. Self-preservation will lead most Chancellors to pursue a shameless charm offensive in the face of this threat.

6 The others

Wealthier countries generally feel it incumbent on them to support economic development in the Third World by providing them with aid, loans, debt relief, disused Greyhound buses, Kalashnikovs, toxic waste... Occasionally Chancellors, overcome with jetlag, will see fit to trim their economic policies in response to decisions on these matters made in international groups. Generally, though, they will duck and weave, and return from these overseas beanos resolute in their determination only to do exactly what is needed to win the next election, which, you must never forget, is precisely what they're there for.

How (not) to manage the economy

Managing the economy is all about making choices: whether to forego butter today for jam tomorrow. Whatever route is taken, there will always be other paths that could have been chosen – the choice not made being the **opportunity cost** of the one that was. Before launching into all this it is worth pausing to consider what different types of economy there are since, though all are made up of markets, societies vary in how far they will let them off the leash.

1 Command economy

At one extreme are the 'command' economies, where all decisions about what will be produced, how much workers will be paid, and when, where and for what price goods are sold are taken by central technocrats who may or may not have any understanding of economics. The most successful ones generally don't.

Command economies were a particular feature of the Communist Block prior to 1989. As these economies did not allow normal market mechanisms such as price adjustments to operate, they instead perfected the art of queuing as their main allocation mechanism. This at least had the advantage that approximately half the adult population was gainfully employed for most of the day.

2 Free market economy

At the other extreme are the 'free market' economies – the stuff of the American dream – where unfettered market forces are given free rein, and life is a bit of a jungle. Free marketeers (not to be confused with three musketeers) eschew regulation or any kind of interference with prices or other market mechanisms and believe that public sector provision and ownership should be kept to an absolute minimum.

3 Mixed economy

Most current industrialized economies have in practice adopted a happy compromise between these two extremes, known as the 'mixed economy', with its balance of public sector, private sector and voluntary (or 'not for profit') provision.

The public sector, unsurprisingly, provides public services from a long menu including education, health care, pensions and welfare benefits, defence, road diggers and bobbies on the beat – anything that a society agrees it wants (apart, that is, from bureaucrats) but not necessarily things that people would want to or be able to buy for themselves.

The private sector is then given a shot at all the rest, and is left relatively well alone, providing it doesn't overstep the mark. The voluntary sector, which relies either on unpaid or non-profitable work, and includes charities, trusts, etc., does all the things that the public sector can't afford to pay for and the private sector can't make a profit out of. A sector with a future, then.

The main thing you need to know, once you have grasped this overall framework, is that the Chancellor (informed by his democratic mandate, of course) has to pull off the following tricks:

a) getting the dosh to pay for the public sector;
b) keeping the economy afloat – which also helps with (a),
c) stopping people doing things they like and encouraging them to do things they don't.

Getting the dosh

The public sector, which in the U.K. adds up to about one-third of the entire economy, is paid for out of taxation, plus any money the government can extract in dental charges or prescription fees, and what they raise from premium bonds or 'gilts' – government stocks, supposedly gold-edged because they are secured crown property.

Despite all these sources of income, Chancellors spend a good deal of time worrying about how they are going to pay the bills. They have to decide not just how much they are going to raise in taxes (a tricky business in itself) but who their prime target will be (a far more risky pursuit).

Some opt for a system where tax rates get progressively higher the more you earn, famously described by one British Chancellor, Denis Healey, as "squeezing the rich until the pips squeak". Others opt for taxes that are the same for everyone – TV licences or car tax for instance. The bluffer must be able to distinguish these by their formal labels of 'progressive taxation' (where the greater your means the more you pay), and 'regressive taxation' (where equal treatment means that the less well-off pay a greater proportion of their income in tax than the rich). However, taxation is far more complicated than just how progressive the tax system is. Among others, there are taxes on:

- income ('direct' taxes, which may or may not be progressive),
- spending ('indirect' taxes, which are basically regressive),
- business ('corporation' taxes),
- car ownership, air travel, and (just to get you one last time),
- death.

A key preoccupation of all Chancellors is to think up ever more innovative and imaginative taxes to spring on the increasingly sceptical public. The trick is to stick to ones that don't include the word tax in their title: call it excise duty or national insurance and people will pay up like lambs.

The Chancellor is unlikely to pay all the bills from money coming in to the Treasury coffers. Not to be outdone by the voracious borrowing of the population he has his own version of overdraft with a budget deficit formerly named the Public Sector Borrowing Requirement, now cunningly re-badged as the **Public Sector Net Cash Requirement (PSNCR)***.

Usually a few billion in the red, the Chancellor, like everyone else, makes regular payments on this debt, trying to keep the balance as low as possible, particularly when interest rates are high. Fortunately for him he pays the Bank of England Interest Rate, not those of credit card companies.

Staying afloat

The better the economy performs, the easier it is for the Chancellor to find the money he needs to pay his bills, and the happier the population is likely to be with their own share of the proceedings. Steering the right course for the economy, then, is at the core of the Chancellor's role, making sure that the economy reaches its destination whilst avoiding the rocks of inflation or the doldrums of recession on the way.

In setting his course, the Chancellor will, above all, need a ship and crew in tip-top condition. For an economy this means that the underlying workings must be basically sound – an economy that tips into inflation at the merest push, or cannot step up a gear without running low on oil isn't going to get very far. Economic policy has, therefore, increasingly focused on getting the fundamentals right. In bluff-speak this is termed **supply side** economics.

Supply side economics focuses on the ingredients that go into the pot to make up the productive side of the economy. It is concerned with the micro-economy, the detailed working of markets, all with the aim of delivering increased competitiveness and productivity and, ultimately, stable and sustainable economic growth. It includes:

* PSNCR has a little sibling called PSNB (don't ask). The thing for bluffers to grasp if making this a special subject is that when the Government sells a tank or a teapot the PSNCR improves, but the PSNB doesn't.

- Freeing up protected markets to competition (as happened in the U.K. with optical products. Now when you buy aspirin for your headache you can get a pair of spectacles over the counter as well);

- Stamping down on uncompetitive pricing so you have no need to buy a less expensive foreign car abroad along with your duty free.

- Making sure that the population is up to speed with the 3Rs, that colleges and universities are heaving with students and that business schools are churning out whizz kid managers and entrepreneurs;

- Encouraging investment, innovation, adoption of new technologies and up-to-date working practices, i.e. ending the tea break.

After lunch, when they have dealt with the supply side, Chancellors move on to the overall strategy for the macro-economy – delivering growth, wealth and contented voters. The competent bluffer must, therefore, be familiar with the levers that Chancellors have for steering the macro-economy. These are basically of two types:

- levers of **fiscal policy** (taxation and government spending on the white elephants of the moment)
- levers of **monetary policy** (control of money and interest rates by committees of the wise and wonderful).

These days governments tend to be rather cautious in their approach to these levers, which is just as well considering the turbulent history of the two opposing schools of thought on their appropriate use.

In the left corner were the **Keynesians** who traditionally focused on fiscal policy to knock the economy back into shape when it veered too far off course. Keynesian

Chancellors believed they could (and should) counteract changes in the overall level of demand for economic output (see economic cycle), by adjusting levels of government spending or taxation accordingly. All bluffers worth their salt should be able to recognise this as the counter-cyclical, or stop-go, demand management that it is.

You may also want to point out that this is not the only rabbit that they tried to pull out of the hat. Demand management was also believed to set up a sort of chain-reaction, known as 'the multiplier effect'. The argument goes that when there is an increase in demand, for instance by the government creating jobs in a depressed area, this doesn't just provide wages for the lucky few. As they spend their wages in local shops, shopkeepers increase their income, suppliers to shopkeepers up their output, and all these people in turn take on more staff and go out and spend more themselves. So, like rabbits multiplying, the effect continues, creating the **virtuous circle** of growth with which Keynesianism has become associated and with which all bluffers should be familiar*.

You will suspect that there must be a catch in all this, otherwise we'd all be Keynesians. Enter right, the **Monetarist**. Monetarists argue that demand management is ultimately futile because it will simply lead to higher prices and not higher output – an observation apparently lent support by the surges in inflation that afflicted Western economies during the heyday of Keynesianism.

Monetarists, logically enough, favoured Monetary policy, rather than targeted interventions, to bring about their desired state of stability and predictability in all things economic. Their principal tenet was that the **money supply** (that is the amount of money in circulation in the

* You might care to picture the opposite effect, when a factory closes and a negative multiplier, akin perhaps to myxematosis, produces a vicious cycle of falling demand.

economy) must be controlled so that it grows only at the same rate that output is growing. Anything faster would simply lead to inflation. Early illustrations of this theory used the metaphor of a helicopter dropping ten pound notes on the population to represent excess printing of money. As soon as people picked up the money, it was argued, they would promptly spend it (what else would you do?), pushing up demand and hence, inevitably prices.

When Monetarism started to be practised in a big way in the 1970s and '80s, economists began to admit, somewhat disconcertingly, that they were not entirely sure what money was (though no doubt they would have recognised it if it had fallen out of the sky).

Some argued for a 'narrow' definition of money, just what you would keep in your pocket or biscuit tin, while others thought that 'broader' definitions including anything vaguely liquid – current accounts, interest accounts, the proceeds of the bring and buy sale, and the beer kitty at work – should be counted. The money supply acquired labels ranging from M_0 to M_4 to cater for all these views, with definitions expanding like an outlandish motorway system. Confused Chancellors went careering down one or other of these routes to monetary control, desperate to pick the one that would get them there fastest, until finally they jumped ship deciding that controlling interest rates, not money, was the only hope of salvation – a position still held by many today.

Declare yourself agnostic about whether it was Monetarism or the high levels of unemployment that accompanied it that ultimately took the inflationary steam out of the economies to which it was applied, and leave yourself space to form your own view of the competing approaches to steering the macro-economic ship. You will be in good company if, in the end, you agree with the wit who said that all economists really do is spend their time re-arranging the deckchairs on the Titanic.

Being nanny

The Chancellor also uses his powers over the nation's purse strings as a way of manipulating behaviour (in everyone's best interests of course). For instance, society may decide that smoking and drinking are bad for people but that having more babies would be a jolly good thing. Whilst Nanny can merely remonstrate with her charges to change their behaviour, a Chancellor can actually make it worth their while. So cigarettes and alcohol are now heavily taxed in most Western countries, reducing the extent to which people indulge in such vices, or at least making it really hurt when they do.

Similarly, pro-natalist governments can offer grants and concessions to encourage women to have more children – France in particular has extensive pre-school childcare and many tax breaks for families with three or more children. It seems that French women are not only falling for this ploy but are also falling pregnant. Figures hot off the press show them outstripping all but the Irish in the Eurobaby contest, with the traditionally fertile, but less well-supported, Italians and Spanish now squeezing in at the bottom.

Taxation and incentives are also used to deal with the problem of **externalities** – things that are produced as a by-product of something else, but for which the perpetrator does not take direct responsibility.

So, for instance, businesses and car users add to pollution and global warming, not necessarily deliberately but inexorably through their lifestyle and consumption choices. Governments will use fines for excessive pollution, taxes on cars and petrol and subsidies for public transport to try and offset this, encouraging people to do less of what is bad and more of what is good. This practice is known, with the economist's usual knack for the slick phrase, as 'internalizing the externalities'.

New Zealand is, it seems, ahead of the herd on this with its vision of a 'cattle tax' to recognise the damaging effect of flatulent cows on global warming by charging farmers for the excess emissions.

Santa's little helpers

Finally, it is time to meet the people who keep the Chancellor's show on the road.

The number crunchers

Stoking up a brew of 'lies, damned lies and statistics' are the statisticians and researchers who collect and analyse data, cursed by a prophecy that foretells that whatever they say, no-one will believe them.

This all begins relatively innocently with a barrage of surveys directed at public agencies, businesses and the populace that probe into matters such as what they had for lunch, how much it cost, and with whom they had it. Once they have elicited the nation's darkest secrets, statisticians will parcel up the information into pretty graphs accompanied by seductive language. Do not be deceived: 'standard deviation', 'Poisson distributions' and 'normal curves' excite no-one but the most committed cruncher.

As a bluffer, you should adopt a pose of mild disdain when confronted with statistics, going on the attack first, particularly if it looks as if they're going to be used to undermine your argument. When others talk about averages buy yourself some time by querying whether this is the **mean** (straight average), **median** (mid-point), or **mode** (simply the most common). And if they claim to have survey data to support them, point out the dangers of the leading question (asking someone if he has stopped bingeing on chocolate pre-supposes he did it in the first place) and the risks of 'response bias' (chocoholics are bound to put your questionnaire in the bin). Don't worry about causing offence

– statisticians deploy very wide confidence intervals (an impressive term for margins of error) in their own defence.

The boffins

Next in the advisory stakes come the boffins, who explain the data. Boffins like nothing better than to blind their audiences with science, and are always on the lookout for people who are not up to speed with things like the difference between **percentage change** and **percentage point change**. If you want to give the impression of effortless mastery of this, the rule of thumb is simple.

If something is measured by a number, as in 10 apples, then change is measured using percentages: 15 apples is a rise of 50%. If something is already a percentage, as in 10% inflation, then it goes up and down in percentage points. An increase to 15% inflation, whilst strictly speaking a rise of 50%, is conventionally described as a rise of 5 percentage points. What it most certainly is not is a rise of 5% as most people seem to think. Never, ever let yourself be caught out on this one, or you will find your façade as a bluffer cracking.

Another favourite boffin foible is to drop the terms 'real' and 'nominal' into the conversation. Again, you cannot afford to be found wanting on this. Just remember that nominal values are given in the prices of the time, whilst real values are adjusted for inflation. So it's no use gasping at how little your Uncle Sid earned when paid £2 a week (the nominal value) for 50 hours cutting out corsets until you know what the real – inflation adjusted – value of £2 would be today.

Exactly the same principle applies when talking about the real and nominal value of output, interest rates, or even your latest pay packet. Note that interest rates are in fact a particularly interesting special case, and a favourite of the boffin who will delight in dangling the brainteaser of **negative real interest rates** in front of you. Nothing impossible about this – when inflation rates rise rapidly as they did in the U.K. in the 1970s they may well be higher than the nominal value of interest rates, which are therefore, perfectly logically, called negative interest rates (really).

The modellers

Extremely clever boffins are allowed to join the elite band of **econometricians**, wizards in the art of applying statistics to economic problems, or, as one commentator has put it, "drawing a crooked line from an unproven assumption to a foregone conclusion". In order to distract themselves from the tedium of all this, econometricians spend most of their time building large models of the economy, becoming very competitive over whose model is best.

As the biggest boy on the block, the Chancellor has the fanciest, known as the Treasury model, and the one that is considered the 'official' model of the economy. This pitches itself against other more or less cheapskate models produced in universities or research institutions.

Bluffers will know that econometricians must get to grips with regression analysis, which shows how closely related (that's 'correlated' to you) two or more economic events (or 'variables') are. Even when they have mastered their dependent and independent variables, spurious correlation and data-mining, they will come up against the ultimate test. This is to account for why no group of econometricians has ever been able to reach the Holy Grail – a model that gives correct predictions about what is going to happen.

In reality it is impossible to make accurate predictions of specific events in economic affairs (although that has never stopped people from trying). Economics may claim to be a scientific, highly evolved subject with models to explain exactly what will happen in a specific set of circumstances. But bluffers will point out that with science things need to be infinitely replicable and nothing in economics ever is. From this it follows, as J.K. Galbraith remarked, that there are only two types of forecaster in economics: those who don't know and those who don't know they don't know.

You might also add that even the most successful of predictions ultimately contains the seeds of its own destruction. The economic model is an Oracle that tells the Chancellor that if one doesn't do this or that then one is set on a course for disaster. When he reacts by doing things differently, the hypothetical disaster doesn't happen. In other words, where predictions are designed to cause a change in policy, the prediction, if acted upon, will appear to have been wrong. Unlike the situation facing the unfortunate Oedipus, economic predictions are, therefore, examples of the self-unfulfilling prophecy.

CHOOSING YOUR STYLE

The great attraction of being a bluffer in economics is that is does not constrain you at all – you can be whatever sort of economist you choose. It is a well-known fact that no two economists will ever agree on anything if they can possibly avoid it: as George Bernard Shaw observed, if all economists were laid end to end, they would never reach a conclusion. So feel free to choose your style from the following identikits.

Hard-nosed business type
An essentially practical brand of economist, concerned with the harsh realities of surviving in the 'real world' and with little patience for the lame ducks of life. Believes in efficiently functioning markets where business knows best. Will there-

fore hold that government should be encouraged to stay out of the market and off his/her back as far as possible. May also be an advocate for the Davids of the small business world against the Goliaths of state monopoly and multinational power. Will be in favour of sound money and low inflation and thus probably tend to favour Monetarism over other types of macro-economic policies that might have more of a people focus.

Woolly liberal with a social conscience

A caring type who will approach economics with a distinctively sociological leaning. Will want to balance environmental and social concerns against the ravages of market forces. May take on the role of a latter-day Keynesian, arguing for state support for employment. Also likely to favour high state investment in health and education, broad-based welfare payments and a guaranteed minimum wage for those left behind in the economic race. All motherhood and apple pie stuff, providing you can pay the bill at the end of it.

Earnest mathematician

Will love the harmony of the mathematical equations and economic models that abound in economics textbooks. Will always be seeking formal proofs of this or that new theory and be keen to demonstrate how much of economics can be reduced to the eloquence of a mathematical expression. Will understand the minutiae of econometric modelling and how the principles of matrix algebra can be applied across a range of problems. Unlikely, though, to get his or her nose out of books for long enough to have many views on practical issues of economic policy.

Renaissance man

Knows a little about a lot of things but not much about anything in particular. With his broad liberal education and grounding in the Classics, Renaissance Man will have loudly-expressed views on the history and philosophy of economics, whilst in practice knowing almost nothing about the subject itself. Entirely undeterred by this small detail, he will enter into arcane debates about the nature of cause and effect – how people can be sure that this or that theory or policy is really all it's cracked up to be. He will avoid maths at all costs, affecting an air of incredulity at any suggestion that this might supplant rhetoric and debate as a tool of economic reasoning.

Radical Marxist

A bit of a maverick and misfit, the radical Marxist, like the Millennialists, is still predicting the Day of Judgement for capitalism, when the workers shall inherit the earth (not literally, of course, as private ownership will have been abolished). Not much sign of the Horses of the Apocalypse at present, but odds on that they could be in for a pretty profit at the 3:30 at Newbury.

ECONOMICS IN THE REAL WORLD

The real fun of being a bluffer is being able to sound at ease when tackling even the most intractable of economic issues. So here are a few of those that are endlessly debated around the world, but which, almost by their very nature, defy resolution. For you the task is to be equipped to join in this debate, recognising that the enjoyment is in the chase: setting out your stall, teasing out the arguments and, when occasion demands, locking horns with the opposition.

You should by now have the tools you need to present the economic rationale for almost any opinion you could possibly hold, safe in the knowledge that as economist Dr Diane Coyle perceptively observed, 'where economics and common sense clash, economics wins every time'.

Globalisation

A term exported by the Americans to represent the phenomenon whereby everything becomes the same the world over, first observed by those eating a Big Mac who had forgotten which country they were in.

With the breaking down of international economic barriers and the power of instant telecommunications, globalisation allows investment and production to move to wherever is cheapest or most profitable, meaning lower prices and cheap things 'made in china' as multi-nationals move in for the kill. Western countries which keep children in the classrooms wearing trainers instead of in the sweatshops stitching them, compete as 'knowledge-based' or 'high-value added' economies in this global melting pot.

Impossible as it is for even the most committed Canute to turn back the tide of globalisation, the debate over how to mitigate its worst effects and make everyone a winner will eddy around for many years yet.

Sustainability

Put at its most simple, this is about making sure that actions taken today don't mess things up for tomorrow. It's a bit like not taking the last biscuit (unless no-one else is looking, of course).

The nub of the argument is that if people continue depleting the world's limited supplies of oil, coal, trees, litter-free beauty spots, caviar, cod, vintage wine, and heating up the planet in the process, they will kill the goose that lays the golden egg.

Although not that many people will now dispute this thesis on a rational level (and if you meet one you can dismiss them with disdain), it has proved a lot harder for consumers, companies and governments to overcome the urge to sneak the last biscuit.

For richer for poorer

Inequality between the 'haves' and 'have nots' is not always a bad thing for an economy – it can be important to create incentives for high fliers to risk everything in the pursuit of fame and riches, making not just themselves but everyone else better off too. This is because the wealth of the chosen few will, it is argued, 'trickle down' to fall, refreshingly, on the heads of those below.

However, inequality and poverty may undermine prosperity if those trapped in a cycle of deprivation do not contribute to the economy suffering instead 'economic marginalization' and 'social exclusion'. You might observe that poverty shares one key thing with wealth: it can be inherited.

There is no short answer to that one. Any remedy for its accumulated ills, will, as always, need money. Where better to go for this than to the rich themselves, you might ask. But there's the rub. If the rich are made to pay too much tax some claim they will no longer have any incentive to work, and will spend all day playing golf. It's up to you if you choose to suggest that, since successful business executives are born workaholics, this could be a double bluff.

Social capital

A sustainable society is one that works together for everyone's benefit, rather than being riven by division, or atrophying through apathy. Its basis is social capital, a rejuvenating force generated by community networks bonding together (not as painful or indeed as interesting, as it sounds). In fact, any club or society can inadvertently find itself producing social capital whether it intends to or not – from the Stitch 'n Bitch Group to the Hell's Angels Pensioners' Club.

The bluffer will of course quickly realize that social

capital is not an end in itself, capital being an essentially economic concept. Social capital, can therefore be thought of as a kind of reserve of trust or good will (or more usually an agreement made over a pint in the pub) that helps communities and businesses to thrive. It's a bit like "You scratch my back, and I'll scratch yours". What might seem a startlingly obvious insight in fact overturns more than a century of received wisdom amongst economists in which the self-centred individualist prospered at the expense of others (presumably just putting up with having an itchy back).

What price health?

Bluffers should make sure they quote Fletcher's Law* here. This states that of the three desirable features of a health service – that it should be Good, Cheap and Fast – it is logically only possible to have two of these at the same time.

- If a health service is both Good and Cheap, then it will inevitably be Slow, as that is the only way that the money can be eked out.
- If it is Cheap and also Fast, then there is bound to be some corner-cutting going on so it won't be Good.
- If society chooses what everyone claims they want – a health service that is both Good and Fast – then it will have to bite the bullet and go for Expensive.

In the countries that have in fact opted for just that: Good, Fast and Expensive, health services are mostly directly charged for, so only affordable to those who can pay, or more

* After a certain Dr. Fletcher, another obscure theorist that no-one will own to not having heard of. Fletcher admits to pinching the idea from a software expert called Reselman who said he pinched it from a Hollywood film director, who apparently didn't pinch anything. A masterly insight, Fletcher's Law can be generalized by adept bluffers to almost any sphere of economics they choose.

usually, their employers. Countries such as the U.K., where services are provided free at the point of delivery (and that's not just maternity services) have by contrast enjoyed provision that is Good and Cheap (because the taxpayer is much stingier than the private buyer), but therefore Slow. This situation seems to have become less acceptable to taxpayers as it dawns on them that there is little point in having a good quality health service if you die whilst waiting your turn.

If forced to take a position on finding the way forward there are really only two possible lines:

1 Everyone gets faster healthcare and society commits to higher taxation. If you support this option you might propose 'hypothecation', where the extra money that people are asked to pay in tax is earmarked (or ring fenced to the bluffer) for that specific purpose.

2 Only the rich get a faster system, in which case they can pay for it privately, and everyone else takes their chance on the waiting list.

The added twist in all this is that the costs of health are set to rise even further as doctors find to their alarm that people have actually listened to their strictures to give up smoking and run round the block twice a day, saving money treating heart attacks now, but stacking up for an extended old age of ailments later.

Will you still feed me?

All bluffers must take a view on the economic ramifications of the dependency debate, the battle for resources between the generations that arises from the boom in the birthrate in the decades after the Second World War just at the point when life-expectancies were soaring to an all-time high. Worse still, these baby boomers became the 'never had it so good' consumer generation who decided to limit themselves to one or two accessory babies and leave it at that. This means that economies are finding themselves with a small number of hard-working young people not only supporting an army of rudely-healthy elders, but also doubly penalized as pension companies rush to shut the stable door after the horse has bolted.

Take sides (using your age as a guide) on the options that Governments have to reduce the burden of high dependency:

a Raising the retirement age to delay the date at which pensions fall due;

b Targeting state pensions on the most needy to cut down on the cost;

c Relaxing restrictions on economic immigrants who can share the pain of paying for pensions;

d Encouraging everyone (especially the young) to save for retirement, hence taking the weight off the state.

Ultimately, though, you might wryly observe that the only real solution for anyone under 40 who still has the energy is to take matters into their own hands and have as many children as possible in a last ditch attempt to turn the dependency ratio back in their favour.

It may be that, in 'the long-run', economists will find answers to even these concerns over health, wealth and the other so-called 'wicked issues'. However, if you have learned anything, it is that though you won't be around for the long-run, at least you are now primed to take your seat at the economists' table. Remember you have one fail-safe Houdini-like egress. If trapped on the wrong end of an un-winnable argument, just side with John Maynard Keynes and nonchalantly declare, as he did, "I'd rather be vaguely right than precisely wrong".

BAFFLING LAWS AND CONCEPTS

A marvellous antidote to the preceding discussion and just the ticket for bluffers wishing to cultivate an air of mild eccentricity. These little gems are of no practical use whatsoever, but will nevertheless, if used in the right company and with the right air of authority, cement your reputation as a bluffer of distinction.

Giffen goods

An interesting phenomenon, allegedly first observed by Sir Robert Giffen (1837-1910) in which people, apparently irrationally, will purchase more of certain goods as soon as their prices rises. A number of possible explanations have been put forward for this, such as:

- A bizarre paradox, fatally misunderstood by queen Marie-Antoinette, which means that if the price of staples such as bread goes up you can't also afford to eat cake, so you eat twice as much bread instead.
- The observation that people who want to be seen 'conspicuously consuming' very flash items, actually prefer their purchases to be as expensive as possible so that they can be as conspicuous as possible.*
- A shocking decline in the nation's mathematical skills.

Cobweb theorem

This shows the tangled web that supply and demand curves get enmeshed in when there is a time lag between a change in price and a resulting change in production or supply. It is traditionally illustrated with reference to the hog market, where the time it takes for a twinkle in the sire's eye to

* Any bluffer unlucky enough to use this particular example in the presence of a boffin after a bad night will soon know that technically these are Veblen goods (after one Thorstein Veblen), not Giffen goods (after Sir Robert), but, hey, no-one else loses sleep over it.

become a fully-fattened pig on the platter is too long for the market. As prices gyrate up and down, increasingly frustrated butchers, farmers and hogs alternately expand and restrict production, chasing their tails as they attempt to keep up with the market. A perfect vehicle for economists to demonstrate their technical drawing abilities, it is now of academic interest only, being one of the many casualties of the invention of the deep freeze.

Fallacy of the lump of labour

Though it might sound like a sort of phantom pregnancy, this is the seemingly simple idea that there is always a fixed amount of work to be done – the lump of labour. While housewives have always known this to be a lie, economists have shown that it is also a fallacy. They argue that you can't just change how all the work in the economy is shared out, for instance by reducing the working week for everyone in work and expecting employers to take on the unemployed to finish things off. Any office worker will tell you that whatever hasn't been done by Friday afternoon will just go in the bin.

Say's law

Academic interpretations of this seminal French theory were initially hampered by poor linguistic skills, with early translators holding that it simply asserted that 'if a good is sold, someone must have bought it'. As people began to realise this was too ludicrous even for the continental school, the theory was eventually refined to the more suitably enigmatic 'supply creates its own demand'. Whilst this principle is clearly exemplified by the fashion industry's facility to generate hysteria over some of the more inexplicable garments of our time, it is reasonable to ponder aloud whether these economists had really thought through other more tricky examples, such as effluent, or school cabbage.

Iron law of wages

This is the proposition that wages will always fall to subsistence level. Clearly if they fall below that level the unfortunate individual will starve. It is also argued that if they rise above that level, competition and market forces will force them back down again. Point out that this theory did overlook just one small thing, the potential of organised labour – guilds and trade unions, plus the restricted entry professions – doctors, accountants and lawyers, to turn this on its head. And in the case of lawyers to establish the precedent that subsistence must include not simply the daily bread, but yachts and holidays in the Caribbean.

Nash equilibrium

Another illustration of how useful game theory can be to real life situations. It looks at the choice faced by someone who knows, for example, that everyone else in the country drives on the left hand side of the road, and who now has to decide whether or not to do the same. For 99.9% of the planet the relevant considerations would include loss of licence, sundry body parts, the relative attractiveness of hospital food, etc. Not so for the economist. It is the disincentive of being in Nash disequilibrium that will clinch the decision.

Shadow prices

For reasons that have never quite been clear, economists are deeply troubled by the fact that the price a particular good is sold for may be different from the price of some other non-existent good that could have been produced using the same inputs. This is believed to offend in some way against the principle of perfectly-functioning markets. To overcome this little local difficulty, economists produced an ingenious new concept – the notion of 'shadow prices'. This is an entirely fictitious pricing system not actually in use anywhere in the economy, but helpful in every other way.

SOME QUOTES

Economics is ...
Everything we know in a language we don't understand;

The only field where two people can share a Nobel prize for saying opposing things;

To be found in the library – beyond fiction;

The one profession where you can gain great eminence without ever being right.

Reasons to become an economist
You will know tomorrow why the things you predicted yesterday didn't happen today.

When you are in the unemployment queue, at least you will know why you are there.

You can believe that real life is a special case.

You can assume everything, except responsibility.

Mick Jagger and Arnold Schwarzenegger studied economics and look how they turned out.

Pearl of wisdom
'There are three things not worth running after: a bus, a woman and a new economic theory. Wait a while and another will come along.'

ex-Chancellor of the Exchequer, Heathcote Amory

And finally ...
How many economists does it take to change a light bulb?

Eight: one to screw it in and seven to hold everything else constant.

None: if it needed changing, market forces would have done it.

One thousand: ten theoretical economists with different theories on how to change the light bulb and 990 empirical economists labouring to determine which theory is the 'correct' one, and everyone will still be in the dark.

GLOSSARY

Autarky A nation's ability to sustain itself without being dependent on trade with others – particularly important during wars when your enemy is unlikely to be sending you the usual supplies of corned beef or condoms.

Budget deficit What happens when a government (or indeed anyone) spends more money than it receives.

Crowding out Conspiracy theory that holds that the public sector is intent on keeping all the best jobs for itself, stifling whatever creativity and initiative the private sector might have had.

Depression The economic equivalent of the psychiatric condition.

Diminishing returns The Skiver's Charter which says that the first five minutes of effort make the most impact, and only suckers carry on after that.

Efficiency wages The practice of paying workers a little bit extra in the hope that they can afford to eat enough to last them until the end of the day.

Elasticity To most people a feature of ageing underwear, to the economist a different measure of stretch, i.e., how far you can push your luck and raise prices before it all pings back in your face and you're left with a pile of pants.

Equilibrium That which is easily lost when trying to get to grips with a micro-economics textbook.

Fiscal drag Not a cross-dressing Chancellor but what happens when a swell of economic growth drags people further than intended into the tax net before the Chancellor has time to release them from the snare.

Free rider Like the housemate who never does the washing up, a parasite who relies on other people's efforts to carry him/her through.

Gini coefficient A measure of all the inequalities bottled up across the world for thousands of years.

Hedging A protective barrier against currency movements allowing exporters to have their cake and eat it.

Hyperinflation An extremely excitable variant of inflation, often requiring wheelbarrows in place of wallets.

Hysteresis Not a panic attack, but the theory that if you didn't get a job when you had the chance you won't be able to get one now. On second thoughts ...

Inferior goods All those things you'd rather not buy the moment you can afford something better; e.g., spam as opposed to ham.

Invisibles Anything that can't be seen as it passes in or out of the country, possibly the odd tax evader, but mainly financial or insurance services, foreign aid, overseas earnings from investing the profits of Harry Potter.

Keynesians Those who believe that government intervention will lead to better economic outcomes. Their doctors are keeping them on the pills.

Marginal cost The additional cost of producing one extra item, leaving aside the sunk costs. Frequently low or even zero, e.g., the cost of making one extra widget.

Monetarists Those who believe that money supply growth is the main cause of inflation. Many of them also believe in UFOs, and some have even seen the Tooth Fairy.

Moral hazard The temptation to behave irresponsibly as soon as you have insured yourself against the consequences.

Opportunity cost What else you could have done with your money/time/life if you hadn't made the decisions you have. Don't believe anyone, Chancellor or otherwise, who says, 'Je ne regret rien.'

Purchasing power parity The proposition that any item – a meal out, a new suit, a bottle of suntan lotion – will cost the same the world over when converted back to your own currency. Not true – it is always more expensive abroad.

Ratchet effect A peculiar economic law that means that whatever goes up will never come down.

Recession As with a receding hairline, a rapid dropping off in output that signals the end of all hope of future growth.

Regression What happens to most students' brains when asked to study econometrics.

Satisficing The schoolboy practice, seen throughout much of industry, of doing exactly enough to get you by, but never any more unless you're really up against it.

Seasonally adjusted figures Statistics that have been 'adjusted' to take account of seasonal factors, such as the increased demand for balls during Wimbledon fortnight.

Stagflation A nasty morning after feeling when the economy experiences everything in slow motion, even though its head is still dizzy with inflation.

Trickle-down effect In the words of J.K. Galbraith, feeding the horse more oats in the hope that some will pass through to the road for the sparrows.

Zero sum game An unnecessarily complicated way of saying that if I win, you loose, and vice versa.

THE AUTHOR

Hilary Cooper studied economics and philosophy which was enough to put her off academic pursuits for life. The dictates of economic rationality should have propelled her straight from a Masters in Economics at Cambridge to a lucrative career in the City. Instead she chose to work in the public sector where she could achieve burn-out by working equally long hours for much less pay, and add unpaid work bringing up a family to her lifetime income stream.

After ten years as an economist in Whitehall she took the well-trodden path of senior professionals into management. She now works for the Government Office for the East of England (an organisation whose purpose remains a closely-guarded secret) where she spends her time collecting increasingly improbable job titles ranging from Deputy Director, Local Area Agreements to Director, Regional Strategy and Corporate Development.

She made the astute move of marrying a population expert with several publications on reproductive behaviours under his belt. The couple have produced three sons, providing her with the constant challenge of ensuring that the supply of food, clothing, sticking-plasters, tranquillizers and gin keeps pace with its rate of consumption.

Further titles in the Bluffer's® Guide series:
www.bluffers.com